P9-DFL-162

Weekly Reader Books presents

Handling Your Disagreements

A Children's Book about Differences of Opinion

by

Joy Wilt

Illustrated by Ernie Hergenroeder

Educational Products Division
Word, Incorporated
Waco, Texas

Author

JOY WILT is creator and director of Children's Ministries, an organization that provides resources "for people who care about children"—speakers, workshops, demonstrations, consulting services, and training institutes. A certified elementary school teacher, administrator, and early childhood specialist, Joy is also consultant to and professor in the master's degree program in children's ministries for Fuller Theological Seminary. Joy is a graduate of LaVerne College, LaVerne, California (B.A. in Biological Science), and Pacific Oaks College, Pasadena, California (M.A. in Human Development). She is author of three books, *Happily Ever After, An Uncomplicated Guide to Becoming a Superparent*, and *Taming the Big Bad Wolves*, as well as the popular *Can-Make-And-Do Books*. Joy's commitment "never to forget what it feels like to be a child" permeates the many innovative programs she has developed and her work as lecturer, consultant, writer, and—not least—mother of two children, Christopher and Lisa.

Artist

ERNIE HERGENROEDER is founder and owner of Hergie & Associates (a visual communications studio and advertising agency). With the establishment of this company in 1975, "Hergie" and his wife, Faith, settled in San Jose with their four children, Lynn, Kathy, Stephen, and Beth. Active in community and church affairs, Hergie is involved in presenting creative workshops for teachers, ministers, and others who wish to understand the techniques of communicating visually. He also lectures in high schools to encourage young artists toward a career in commercial art. Hergie serves as a consultant to organizations such as the Police Athletic League (PAL), Girl Scouts, and religious and secular corporations. His ultimate goal is to touch the hearts of kids (8 to 80) all over the world—visually!

This book is a presentation of Weekly Reader Books.
Weekly Reader Books offers book clubs for children from
preschool through junior high school.

For further information write to:
WEEKLY READER BOOKS
1250 Fairwood Ave.
Columbus, Ohio 43216

Handling Your Disagreements

Copyright © 1980 by Joy Wilt. All rights reserved. Printed in the United States of America. No part of this book may be used or reproduced in any manner whatsoever without written permission, except in the case of brief quotations embodied in critical articles and reviews. This edition is published by arrangement with Educational Products Division, Word, Incorporated, 4800 West Waco Drive, Waco, Texas 76710.

ISBN: 0-8499-8141-7
Library Of Congress Catalog Card Number: 79-53572

Janet Gray, Editor

The educational concepts presented in the Ready-Set-Grow book series are also featured in a music songbook and longplay record. For further information concerning these materials see your local bookstore or write Word, Incorporated, 4800 West Waco Drive, Waco, Texas 76710.

6 7 8 9 / 86 85 84

Contents

Introduction

<u>Handling Your Disagreements</u> is one of a series of books.   The complete set is called *Ready-Set-Grow!*

<u>Handling Your Disagreements</u> deals with solving conflicts and can be used by itself or as a part of a program that utilizes all of the *Ready-Set-Grow!* books.

<u>Handling Your Disagreements</u> is specifically designed so that children can either read the book themselves or have it read to them.   This can be done at home, church, or school.   When reading to children, it is not necessary to complete the book at one sitting. Concern should be given to the attention span of the individual child and his or her comprehension of the subject matter.

<u>Handling Your Disagreements</u> is designed to involve the child in the concepts that are being taught. This is done by simply and carefully explaining each concept and offering guidelines that the child can apply in his or her own life.

Handling Your Disagreements shows children how poorly handled disagreements can lead to arguments, fights, and scapegoating. It offers guidelines that can help children think creatively in order to come to positive resolutions of their conflicts.

Handling Your Disagreements teaches that conflicts do not always have to end with one person "winning" and the other "losing." Nor does a disagreement always mean that one person is "right" and the other "wrong." In fact, disagreements that are dealt with carefully can help people learn and grow. Children who grow up understanding this concept will be better equipped to live healthy, fulfilling lives.

6

Handling Your Disagreements

You are a person living with other people. Because this is true . . .

you will have disagreements.

9

What does this mean?

To help you understand what a disagreement is . . .

11

This is Diane and Lydia. They are best friends.

Diane and Lydia take turns playing at each other's house.

One day, it was Diane's turn to go to Lydia's house. As Diane walked into Lydia's yard, she looked down and found a crumpled dollar bill on the ground.

Diane picked up the dollar. For the next hour, the girls went all over the neighborhood, trying to find out if anyone had lost a dollar bill.

When no one claimed the money, Diane decided to keep it, since she had found it.

Lydia didn't agree with Diane's decision.

The two girls saw the same situation differently. Diane had one idea about who the dollar should belong to, and Lydia had a different idea about who the dollar should belong to.

Diane and Lydia disagreed.

Diane tried to convince Lydia that she was right, and Lydia tried to convince Diane that she was right. The girls began to argue. Each girl said what she thought and how she felt without trying to understand what the other girl thought and felt.

21

Neither girl felt she was being listened to, so they both became very angry.

They began to fight. They tried to hurt each other.

23

Lydia's mother heard the girls fighting. She stepped in
to stop the fight.

Needless to say, both Diane and Lydia lost.

Like Diane and Lydia, you too will experience disagreements. But you don't have to lose.

Disagreements don't have to turn into arguments and fights. They can help you learn and grow . . . that is, if they are understood and handled wisely.

Chapter 1

Understanding Disagreements

No two people are the same.

Each person is unique in the way he or she looks, acts, feels, and thinks.

Some people think the same way about some things.

But no two people think the same about everything.

Because this is true, there are going to be disagreements among people.

You are a person, and because you are one, you too will have disagreements with other people. How will this make you feel?

If you are like most people, you might find that when you disagree with someone, you have all kinds of uncomfortable feelings.

Disagreeing with someone might make you feel insecure. Feeling insecure means being afraid something bad might happen to you.

It might also make you feel inferior. Feeling inferior means feeling as if you're not as smart or as good as the person you disagree with.

Disagreeing with someone might make you feel unsure of yourself and what you think.

It might also make you feel frustrated.

But no matter how you feel, it's best to bring disagreements out in the open and resolve them. Whenever disagreements are not resolved, several things can happen.

38

39

Sometimes an unresolved disagreement becomes an argument.

Sometimes an unresolved disagreement becomes a fight.

Sometimes, when a disagreement is not resolved, the people who have different opinions stay frustrated and angry and they take their hostile feelings out on someone else.

This is called "scapegoating." Scapegoating is when a person who is involved in a disagreement hurts an innocent person who wasn't involved in the disagreement.

To help you understand what scapegoating means . . .

This is Mr. Brown.

This is Mr. Jones. Mr. Jones is Mr. Brown's boss.

45

Because Mr. Brown and Mr. Jones work together and see each other often, they sometimes disagree.

48

49

Mr. Brown did not resolve his disagreement with Mr. Jones. Instead, he ended up being angry at his wife. Mrs. Brown became Mr. Brown's scapegoat.

Why do you think Mr. Brown couldn't resolve his disagreement with Mr. Jones?

It might have been because Mr. Brown was afraid that if he disagreed out loud with Mr. Jones, he would lose his job. Mr. Brown did not consider Mr. Jones a "safe" person to share his feelings with.

A safe person is someone you can trust not to reject or hurt you when you disagree with them.

Mr. Brown considered Mrs. Brown a safe person, so he made her his scapegoat. This started a chain reaction.

WELL, OF ALL THE NERVE! I SPEND HOURS IN THE KITCHEN COOKING HIS FAVORITE MEAL, AND ALL HE CAN DO IS YELL AT ME!

53

Now look who's scapegoating.

And the scapegoating continues.

57

Unresolved disagreements can cause arguments, fights, and scapegoating, if they are not understood and handled wisely.

A miserable evening in the Brown family could have been avoided, if only Mr. Brown had handled his disagreement with Mr. Jones more wisely.

But before you can handle disagreements wisely, there are several things you need to know.

First of all:

It's OK to disagree with other people.

The second thing you need to know is:

People who disagree with other people are not strange or bad.

EVERYONE IN THE CLASS WANTS TO GO TO THE ZOO EXCEPT DUMB OLD JACOB. HE THINKS WE SHOULD GO TO THE MUSEUM.
SO WHAT? JACOB HAS A RIGHT TO THINK WHATEVER HE WANTS TO THINK. JUST BECAUSE HE DOESN'T AGREE WITH EVERYONE ELSE, THAT DOESN'T MEAN HE'S WEIRD.

The third thing you need to know is:

When most people disagree with a person's ideas, that
doesn't mean the person's ideas are stupid or unimportant.

The fourth thing you need to know is:

When two people disagree, that doesn't always mean one person is right and the other person is wrong.

It's possible for both people to be right. It's also possible
for both people to be wrong.

The fifth thing you need to know is:

Not all disagreements have to end with both people agreeing.

The last thing you need to know about disagreements is:

When people disagree, it doesn't mean they are angry with each other or they don't like each other.

People can disagree and still love, respect, and trust each other.

73

So, before you can resolve disagreements, there are some things you need to know about.

Disagreements are OK.

People who disagree with other people are not strange or bad.

When most people disagree with a person's ideas, that doesn't mean the person's ideas are stupid or unimportant.

When two people disagree, that doesn't always mean one person is right and the other person is wrong.

Not all disagreements have to end with both people agreeing.

When people disagree, that doesn't mean they are angry with each other or they don't like each other.

If you can remember these things, you will be able to handle disagreements wisely.

Chapter 2

Handling Disagreements Wisely

People disagree about many different kinds of things.

Sometimes people disagree about who will take part in an activity.

Sometimes people disagree about what will be done.

Sometimes people disagree about why something should be done.

Some people disagree about when something will happen.

Some people disagree about where something will take place.

Some people disagree about how things should be done.

Besides who, what, why, where, and how, there are many other things people have disagreements about.

But the important thing about disagreements is not what they are about. The important thing is how they are handled.

There are several things you can do to handle disagreements wisely.

STEP ONE: Figure out what the disagreement is about. This means, find out what the other person thinks and what you think, and then decide what it is that you disagree about.

STEP TWO: Listen to the other person and find out why the person thinks the way he or she does.

When you listen to another person, be <u>sure</u> to . . .

>face the person and look directly into his or her eyes, and concentrate on what the person is saying.

Try <u>not</u> to:

>interrupt,
>
>make judgments about what the person is saying before he or she finishes, or
>
>think about anything else.

To do a good job of listening, you need to put yourself in the other person's place and try to understand why the person thinks the way he or she does.

THE LAST TIME WE WENT TO PLAY MINIATURE GOLF, WE HAD TO WAIT IN LINE A WHOLE HOUR. BY THE TIME IT WAS OUR TURN, IT WAS SO COLD WE COULD HARDLY STAND TO BE OUTSIDE. AND I HAVEN'T SEEN A MOVIE FOR A LONG TIME.

Make sure you know why the other person thinks the way he or she does.

STEP THREE: Kindly and honestly tell the other person why you think the way you do.

When you are sure the other person understands what you think . . .

STEP FOUR: Research both opinions.

Find out all you can about what the other person thinks and what you think.

Study and talk to other people about both opinions.

After you find out all you can about both sides . . .

STEP FIVE: Decide together what you should do.
Here are some possible solutions:

You might decide to agree with the other person.

The other person might decide to agree with you.

You can compromise. This means you both give in a little without either of you giving in completely.

You can agree to disagree.

You can agree about something entirely different.

Whether you decide that . . .

you will agree with the other person,

the other person will agree with you,

both of you will compromise,

both of you will agree to disagree, or

both of you will agree about something entirely different . . .

STEP SIX: Do what you have both decided to do.

101

So, if you want to handle disagreements wisely, follow these six steps:

STEP ONE: Figure out what the disagreement is about.

STEP TWO: Listen to the other person and find out why the person thinks the way he or she does.

STEP THREE: Kindly and honestly tell the other person why you think the way you do.

STEP FOUR: Research both opinions.

STEP FIVE: Decide together what you should do.

STEP SIX: Do what you have both decided to do.

If you have a problem doing these things, ask a person you both trust and respect to help you resolve the disagreement.

Disagreements are a normal part of being with other people. But if you aren't careful, they can become arguments and fights. When this happens, someone might get hurt. This is why it's important to make sure your disagreements do not turn into arguments and fights.

Chapter 3

Making Sure Disagreements Do Not Turn Into Arguments or Fights

To make sure disagreements do not turn into arguments or fights, here are some things to try to remember.

1. Don't get into a discussion with another person when you are tired or in a bad mood.

When you are tired or in a bad mood, you might take your feelings out on someone else, making that person your scapegoat.

2. Make sure you and everyone around you understand and agree to the same basic rules that everyone is to live by.

If you are following one set of rules and someone else is following another set of rules, it's more likely that your disagreements will turn into arguments and fights.

When the rules have been discussed and made clear, when everyone agrees and understands them, it is easier to resolve disagreements.

3. Say you're sorry, and really mean it, when you have been wrong.

4. Remember that no one, including you, is perfect. No one is right all the time.

5. Respect other people's opinions.

If you do this, other people will be more likely to respect and accept your opinions.

6. Don't share your thoughts with anyone who does not respect and accept you.

Having your thoughts rejected by someone because they don't respect or accept you might hurt you and cause you to feel bad about yourself.

So, remember these things to make sure your disagreements do not turn into arguments and fights.

1. Don't get into a discussion with another person when you are tired or in a bad mood.

2. Make sure you and everyone around you understand and agree to the same basic rules that everyone is to live by.

3. Say you're sorry, and really mean it, when you have been wrong.

4. Remember that no one, including you, is perfect. No one is right all the time.

5. Respect other people's opinions.

6. Don't share your thoughts and opinions with anyone who does not respect and accept you.

Conclusion

No two people are the same. Every person is unique in the way he or she looks, acts, feels, and thinks.

Because this is true, people have disagreements.

You are a person, and because you are one, you too will have disagreements with other people.

If you are like most people, you might find that when you disagree with someone, you have all kinds of uncomfortable feelings. You might feel insecure, inferior, unsure of yourself, and frustrated.

But no matter how you feel, it's best to bring disagreements out in the open and resolve them.

Unresolved disagreements can lead to arguments, fights, and scapegoating. When this happens, someone might get hurt.

Before you can resolve disagreements, there are some things you need to know about.

Disagreements are OK.

People who disagree with other people are not strange or bad.

When most people disagree with a person's ideas, that doesn't mean the person's ideas are stupid or unimportant.

When two people disagree, that doesn't always mean one person is right and other person is wrong.

Not all disagreements have to end with both people agreeing on the same thing.

When people disagree, that doesn't mean they are angry with each other or they don't like each other.

Then, to help you resolve disagreements, there are six steps to follow.

STEP ONE: Figure out what the disagreement is about.

STEP TWO: Listen to the other person and find out why he or she thinks the way he or she does.

STEP THREE: Kindly and honestly tell the other person why you think the way you do.

STEP FOUR: Research both opinions.

STEP FIVE: Decide together what you should do.

STEP SIX: Do what you have both decided to do.

And finally, to make sure that your disagreements do not turn into arguments or fights, keep in mind these things.

1. Don't get into a discussion with another person when you are tired or in a bad mood.

2. Make sure you and everyone around you understand and agree to the same basic rules that everyone is to live by.

3. Say you're sorry, and really mean it, when you have been wrong.

4. Remember that no one, including you, is perfect. No one is right all the time.

5. Respect other people's opinions.

6. Don't share your thoughts and opinions with anyone who does not respect and accept you.

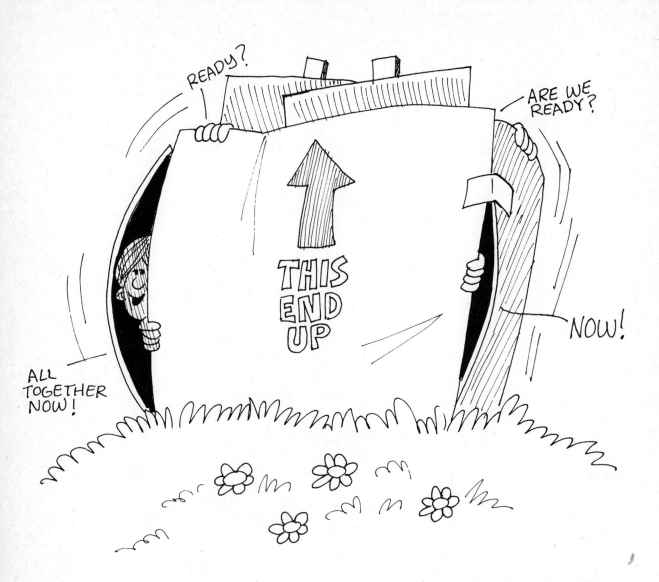

So remember . . .